Sexual Abuse of Children
Understanding, intervention and prevention

Edited by Diana Riley, Consultant Psychiatrist
St John's Hospital, Aylesbury

Translated from the original by Jacqueline Rutgers,
Pro Juventute, Zürich

Radcliffe Medical Press
Oxford

English translation © 1991 Radcliffe Medical Press Ltd
15 Kings Meadow, Ferry Hinksey Road, Oxford OX2 0DP

British Library Cataloguing in Publication Data

Sexual abuse of children: understanding, intervention and
prevention.
  1. Children. Sexual abuse by adults
  I. Riley, Diana.   II. [A leurs corps defendant]. *English*
362.76

ISBN 1 870905 76 8

Printed and bound in Great Britain by Bocardo Press,
Oxford
Typeset by Advance Typesetting Ltd, Oxford

© Verlag Pro Juventute, Zurich 1990

Contents

Acknowledgements

My most grateful thanks are due to Seymour Major of Blackman and Blackman, Solicitors, Harrow, Middlesex, and to David King and Carla Healey of the Solicitors Department, Buckinghamshire County Council for their knowledgeable advice on the legal aspects of this book.

Also to: Mrs Valerie Cahill and Linda Brennan, librarians at St John's Hospital, Stone, Aylesbury, Bucks, and Martin Tapsell, Bibliography Section, Buckinghamshire Library Headquarters, Aylesbury for their invaluable help with the bibliography.

I should like to thank Pro Juventute and Jacqueline Rutgers for their permission to use the original work and Linda Parkin for her translation.

Preface

It is interesting to note how recently society has accepted that women and, even more recently, that children have rights. Western culture still seems to regard children as second-class citizens and allows the many injustices committed against them and the suffering they experience to occur in silence and secrecy. These injustices and suffering are partly the consequence of ignorance and shame, which is perhaps excusable, and partly due to conscious indifference, which is not.

Ignorance and shame can be dealt with by education and explanation, and it is this task which is addressed in this book. We hope that it will have a wide circulation, and will help parents, health professionals, lawyers, teachers, social workers, and the police to act in the best interests of children.

It is only recently that the extent of child sexual abuse has become apparent, and it is still impossible to give accurate figures about the incidence. Indications of its frequency are often retrospective, provided by adults who, in psychotherapy, remember and talk about their experiences. This fact alone illustrates the profound and far-reaching effect of such abuse.

The early diagnosis and treatment of the problem requires all adults, especially those concerned with child care and welfare, to be particularly observant. The signs and symptoms are not always very clear, and may be misinterpreted or ignored. The link between a child's disturbed behaviour and possible sexual abuse is not always obvious, as this book clearly explains.

We should all be vigilant, and keep the possibility of sexual abuse in mind when dealing with sad or disturbed children. We should be neither naïve nor afraid. The means for intervention do exist and are slowly improving, as the list of useful literature, videos, and addresses given at the end of this book illustrates.

We are grateful to Pro Juventute for becoming involved in this difficult but necessary battle.

PROFESSEUR P. E. FERRIER
Clinique de Pediatre
Hôpital Cantonal Universitaire
Geneva

Foreword

In this book we hope that you will find clear information on child sexual abuse which we consider should be shared openly.

You will bring your own experience and knowledge to the subject, and you may find what is written here too superficial or too detailed, the tone of the book too outspoken or too reticent. On a subject as sensitive as this, it has been difficult to find a middle course. In fact, even talking about sexual abuse impinges on each individual's personal freedom.

Writing about sexual matters involves writing about an intimacy normally kept private. When it refers to children, it touches a chord in each individual which will resonate differently according to each person's own experience. To write about family life is to enter a private domain.

Faced with the general lack of freely available information, we have chosen to concentrate on informing adults and, in particular, professionals involved with child welfare. In this way we felt that they would be better equipped to help abused children and to provide preventive measures.

Even though victims are now beginning to be traced more readily, the means of dealing with and helping such cases are still inadequate.

We have chosen to avoid the use of case studies. There is a danger of sensationalizing abuse through these, which may detract from our ability to provide means of support for individual victims.

A programme of prevention should be implemented urgently in our schools, and wherever there is contact with young people and families. There are many examples of successful intervention in other countries.

We hope that this book will raise the level of consciousness of our society and its sense of responsibility in trying to help both victims and perpetrators.

We sincerely hope that our experience will encourage others in their professional work, and stimulate further and better-informed discussion.

JACQUELINE RUTGERS
Pro Juventute
Zürich

Introduction

Sexual abuse is only one of the ways in which children are mistreated. It is a reality which is rarely discussed, and which is therefore all the more disturbing. Newspaper and television reports of sexual aggression, the abduction of children, and of incest leave parents and teachers bewildered. They feel impotent in the face of this taboo subject which is seldom tackled in educational literature. Secretly they hope that it happens only to others.

There is a lack of accurate information regarding the incidence of sexual abuse in the UK, but the estimated number of young victims is in the order of 7,000 per year. Cases of incest are almost impossible to quantify.

This book is aimed at parents, teachers, social workers, health professionals, magistrates, lawyers, and the police – in fact anyone who comes into contact with children and undertakes responsibility for them.

This book complements the literature already available to facilitate a dialogue between parents and children. (*See* Resources at the end of the book for further examples.)

Its objectives are:

● to put an end to the silence surrounding sexual abuse, and to help bring it to the attention of families and the public in general;

● to protect children, by going beyond the vague warnings given in the past, giving precise definitions, clear explanations, and practical advice, as well as providing a basis for preventive education;

● to describe how to respond when faced with a case of sexual abuse, whether suspected or confirmed, and what steps to take to help the victim as quickly and effectively as possible.

From the statistics available, more girls than boys are victims of child sexual abuse, and men rather then women the perpetrators of such abuse. For this reason it has been decided to adopt the feminine pronoun when discussing the abused child in this book, and to refer to the abuser as male. It *must* however be remembered that boys can be and are the victims of abuse and this must be borne in mind at *all* times.

1

The Sexual Abuse of Children

What is it all about?

In sexual abuse:

- the abuser is an adult or adolescent who uses a child for a sexual act to satisfy his need for power, bravado, tenderness, and contact as well as his erotic desires, to the detriment of the child;

- the child victim is sexually aroused or drawn into a sexual act, the meaning of which she does not completely understand, and which is inappropriate for her age, her emotional development, and her role within the family. Sometimes she is forced to take part in sexual acts, sometimes to look at pornographic pictures or films.

There is *no* abuse:

- in sexual games between children of similar ages in which there is no force, embarrassment, or suffering. These are innocent explorations linked to the child's search for her own identity. Satisfying this natural curiosity is both healthy and safe.

Comments

Whilst the practice of certain acts which we define as sexual abuse is a reality as old as humanity, these acts have only been described as abuse since the medico-legal literature of the nineteenth century.

Furthermore, we have recognized only recently how devastating its impact can be on the mental health and development of children.

Certain acts which we regard in our society as sexual abuse are considered to be quite normal, even ritualistic, in some cultures. These may be detrimental to the child's normal development, but are less distressing in this context, because these children do not experience the same guilt or feeling of social isolation.

Which acts are involved?

The term sexual abuse covers a wide variety of acts of a sexual nature which are embodied in the Offences Against the Person Act 1861 and the Sexual Offences Act 1965. Sexual abuse may or may not involve some form of physical contact – vaginal, genital, oral, or anal. Some acts directly affect the child's body, some the adult's, others both at the same time.

Some basic definitions:

- *exhibitionism* – sexual deviation in the form of exposure of the (usually male) genital organs. The penis may be flaccid or erect, and the act is sometimes accompanied by masturbation

- *voyeurism* – the search for sexual satisfaction by watching the naked child or sexual acts involving the child

- *fellatio* – introduction of the abuser's penis into the child's mouth or vice versa

- *sodomy* – forced or attempted anal penetration by the abuser

- *paedophilia* – sexual deviation which drives an adult to seek sexual gratification by involving children

- *pederasty* – although this means essentially the same as paedophilia, this word usually refers to male homosexuality between an adult and a child

● *incest* – a sexual act between parent (or step-parent) and child, or between brother and sister. In a wider sense sexual abuse within the family or committed by an adult in the role of parent. *

Prevalence

Prevalence gauges the total percentage of the adult population who have experienced sexual abuse at any time during childhood. Information is therefore only available from adults who later reveal their earlier experience. Various authors have attempted to establish prevalence but have used different definitions of sexual abuse and have studied different sections of the population. In one UK study of female patients in general practice, 42% reported some degree of sexual contact with an adult, and 22% reported physical sexual experiences. In a similar study with female students, the comparable figures were 54% and 28%.

Incidence

The incidence rate is the number of new cases occurring in a population in a single year. There are currently no national statistics for the UK. Some estimate of reported cases only can be gained from figures published by the National Society for the Prevention of Cruelty to Children (NSPCC). In 1989, this organization was notified of 621 cases of sexual abuse to children, together with 24 cases of physical and sexual abuse; 12 cases of neglect and sexual abuse; and 14 cases of neglect, physical and sexual abuse, in the 12 Local Authority areas where they managed the child abuse register. These areas represent 10% of the total child population. By extrapolation therefore, we can estimate that there are more than 6,700 cases of child sexual abuse each year in

---

* Incest is a much more common instance of sexual abuse than is generally recognized. It is common in all classes of society, both urban and rural, and often occurs in subsequent generations. Most commonly cases of incest occur between father and daughter(s), stepfather and stepdaughter(s). The abuser can also be the mother's lover, the victim's teacher, adopted father, grandfather, older brother, or any person closely involved with the family. While the victim can be male, it appears to be less common for the perpetrator to be female.

this country. This figure is certainly an underestimate, since it is known from experience with adults that only a small proportion of cases will have come to light.

The mean age of these sexually abused children was 10 years two months at the time of reporting. Eighteen percent of the sexually abused children were less than five years old, and over 80% were girls.

2

Myths and Realities

Myths

Prejudices and mistaken beliefs abound on the subject of sexual abuse. It is important to understand the facts. Below is a list of common myths.

- Sexual abuse exists only in the child's imagination, particularly with those children who often make up stories, or in the imagination of a particularly anxious parent.

- Even if the child was not imagining what happened, it is of little importance, and she will soon forget.

- All these children are thought to be potential victims:
  - the pretty, neat little girl who is envied by others
  - the charming or cute little girl who appears provocative
  - the little girl who is naïve or unsure of herself, constantly seeking the approval of her elders
  - the disobedient child who wanders from home
  - the neglected child to whom nobody pays attention.

- Children can be protected by warning them to be obedient, sensible, and wary of strangers.

- Parks, public toilets, and deserted streets, particularly after dark, are the only dangerous places.

- Suspicious-looking strangers or old men on their own are the people to be wary of.

- Women do not abuse children sexually.

Realities

Contrary to previously held beliefs, we now know that sexual abuse, and incest in particular, is very common.

Below is a list of realities.

● Children do not generally tell lies about abuse. Cases of making up stories are extremely rare, and express a need for attention which we should try to understand. A first response must be to always believe the child.

● Both the short- and long-term effects of sexual abuse are extremely serious for the emotional and physical health of the child. 'The worst thing in life is that you cannot change your memory,' one seven-year-old girl said, having been raped by her father.

● The facts are that one boy in ten, and one girl in four, have been victims of some form of sexual abuse before reaching adult life. The incidence in psychiatric patients is even higher.

● The victims come from all socio-economic groups. They are most frequently children aged between six and 12 but infants and very small children are also abused, especially in cases of incest.

● Girls seem to be the victims of incest more frequently than boys, but recently it has become clear that boys are more frequently the victims of paedophilia, and are often carefully chosen for their good behaviour and discretion.

● It is not the outward appearance nor the provocative or rebellious behaviour of the child that makes her vulnerable to abuse. Most often the child does not at first understand the abuser's intentions. Even if the child talks and behaves in a provocative way – which she may have learned as a way of expressing her feelings – she is never to blame.

● The location which the abuser prefers is one regularly frequented by the child – school and the surrounding area, the route between school and home, the home of a relative or friend, or the home of the child herself. As far as timing is concerned, the abuser often takes advantage of a moment of relaxation when the child wants to play, or when she is washing or going to bed. In many cases the abuse is repeated.

- In 80–95% of cases the abuser is known to his victim. Apart from his behaviour, there is nothing to distinguish the perpetrator. He is commonly between 20 and 40, married, a father, leading a normal social life, enjoying the respect of his colleagues and friends, and often holding a position of trust and authority in relation to children – in short, a person apparently above suspicion.

- There are far fewer women than men who sexually abuse children. On the other hand, theirs may be a passive or collusive role, failing to put a stop to the abuse for fear of violence or the break-up of the family.

Who is the abuser?

Behind the respected character described above is hidden a timid personality, lacking in self-confidence and self-esteem. He

experiences strong feelings of shame. He is often unable to maintain an equal relationship with adults. He lacks self-control and needs to exert control over others. This is why he chooses as his victims those who are weaker and less mature than himself — he uses the child to increase his own feelings of power. He does not necessarily intend to cause harm or injury, and is often unable to accept that he inflicts suffering on the child.

How does the abuser operate?

The adult abuser resorts to various ways of winning over his victim, taking advantage of her character, her needs, and her particular

circumstances. He attracts her by playing with her, by arousing her curiosity, or by offering presents, rewards, or treats (sweets or toys, outings, money, even shelter for young runaways) in order to persuade her to submit to his demands.

He sees and exploits the need for friendship and attention in the child who is deprived of affection and who has problems at home, perhaps related to a change of school or to a family crisis or illness. He shows her affection, makes her feel that she is special, and gradually wins her confidence.

Whether he has got to know the child and won her confidence or already enjoys her affection as a relative or friend, the abuser then plays his trump card – complicity. In this way he is able to take his time over initiating the child into what he describes as 'their secret game'. He no longer needs to use compulsion. The child is persuaded to accept the need for secrecy, and this makes the abuser feel safe from discovery.

Sometimes the abuser uses an element of surprise, violence, or intimidation. To overcome attempts at resistance, he uses his authority as an adult and his physical superiority, and frightens the child, perhaps threatening to take revenge on her family. He relies on the child's weakness, her confusion, and paralysing terror, playing on his victim's inexperience to convince her that he will carry out his threats.

If the child tries to put a stop to the abuse, the perpetrator usually resorts to blackmail. He convinces the child that people will call her a liar; that she will be ridiculed and rejected, and will lose the affection of her loved ones. He takes advantage of the child's worry, shame, and humiliation at what has happened, and her guilt if she has been disobedient. He makes the victim think that it is her own fault and that she is stupid to have become involved. He may even go so far as to threaten to lock the child up or to commit suicide if disclosures are made. What an effective way of making sure the child remains silent!

3

Trauma and its Consequences

All sexual abuse is psychologically harmful and damages the child to a greater or lesser extent, depending on the circumstances.

It is wrong to pretend that an adult can make a child experience and enjoy sexual feelings. The child is chosen because she is easier to deceive, easier to frighten, easier to dominate and control. The sexual abuse of children is characterized by a combination of four damaging factors which occur in varying degrees and proportions according to the circumstances.

These factors are:

● the sexualization of the relationship between the abuser and the child;

● the betrayal of the child's confidence by the abuser;

● the child's realization of her powerlessness to protect herself;

● the blame and secrecy imposed by the abuser, which isolate the child from her family and peer group.

The harmful effect of these factors colours the child's view of herself and the world, and affects her emotional health and personal relationships, not only at the time but for years afterwards.

The effect that an isolated incident has on a child is generally less than that of a situation which is repeated. Continuing sexual abuse can dominate a child's life for months, even years.

The same abuse will affect individual children differently according to the child's background and personality. The effect will also vary after discovery of the abuse, depending on the reactions of those involved with the child and the actions taken to protect her.

The child is affected differently according to the nature of the abusive act – whether she is herself sexually stimulated or has actively stimulated her abuser, or whether her role is only passive.

The effect of the same abuse also differs according to the age of the child. For example, a child at or past puberty will feel humiliated and violated more readily, will believe more frequently that she is to blame, and will be more embarrassed to talk about it.

The problem increases when the abuse is associated with fear and pain or the pleasure of receiving attention, affection, and treats. The resulting inner conflicts may be long-lasting and deeply harmful. Children who are sexually abused are generally confused in their relationship to adults.

These experiences of abuse leave a distorted view of sexuality, devaluing the victim's image of herself and her attitudes to her body. Sexual feelings can suffer long-term damage as a result of these painful, worrying, or confusing feelings.

The child will feel more betrayed and deceived if the abuser is someone whom she loves and trusts, or if it is someone with whom she had developed a close, warm relationship over a period of time. When the child reveals the abuse, the negative reaction and disbelief of those around her can increase this feeling of betrayal. The child no longer knows whom she can trust.

All children are aware that they cannot always have their own way. But the most paralysing feeling of powerlessness is experienced by the victim of abuse who has been unable to defend herself against the invasion of her body, and who has been forced to keep this dreadful secret. The child who is threatened or who feels trapped by the abuser's domination suffers all the more. This feeling of helplessness is even worse when her attempts to alert those around her or convince them about the abuse are unsuccessful. As a consequence she may feel weak and incapable, and suffer from lack of confidence in later life.

When the abuser humiliates the child and makes her feel that she has done wrong, the child may feel ashamed and worthless. This feeling of guilt forces her to keep silent, and to become even more isolated. The isolation is increased if, when the situation is disclosed, the victim is criticized and rejected by those close to her. Later in life, she lacks self-esteem, feels unworthy of respect, confidence and friendship, and sees herself as different from her peer group.

The effects of this situation may be transitory or lasting, and may be aggravated or diminished by a number of factors. These include:

● the strengths and weaknesses of the child's own personality;

● the strengths and weaknesses of her family support;

● the reaction of those around her to her behaviour, and to what she says;

● what sort of help she is offered.

Incest

We know most about incest from the evidence given by women who have been victims of it in their childhood. We therefore know it to be a serious situation with far-reaching consequences. The child or adolescent victim of incest is locked with her whole family into an unhealthy situation, sometimes repeated over several generations. Mystery, betrayal, confusion, and lies poison the atmosphere, and trust is no longer possible. In some families the model of tenderness between parent and child becomes grotesquely distorted and dominated by abusive behaviour and erotic overtones.

The victim is treated in some ways like an adult, but also like a helpless child. She finds herself trapped in a situation which is taboo – one which involves the family but is also sexual. She cannot escape, even if and when she realizes how she is being exploited. She feels alienated – her silent distress cuts her off from a normal child's life and from all genuine relationships. The secret she must keep involves not only her family but also those around her, and she lives in a permanent state of anxiety. As an involuntary accomplice in a silent conspiracy, she may believe that she alone is responsible for safeguarding the unity of the family.

Parents no longer play a protective role – neither the father, whose power becomes a threat, nor the mother, who is sometimes thought to be an accomplice. Sometimes the mother, distressed by the confessions of her child and reluctant to believe them, reacts by rejecting her. However, many brave mothers recognize how their child is suffering and are able to face up to the situation to do all they can to protect her.

Once the secret is out, it is possible to begin to do something. Everyone can and should be helped, starting with the victim. Suitable therapy should be offered, and often separation should be arranged, wherever possible removing the abuser from the family home rather than the victim.

4

Why does the Child Keep her Secret?

When one grasps what the child goes through in a situation of sexual abuse, it is easier to understand why many children find it almost impossible to talk about what has happened to them, or why they take so long to reveal that they have been abused.

What are the child's reasons for keeping silent?

- The small child does not necessarily understand the fact that she has been abused – particularly if she has been made to feel that it was a game, or if she cannot put what happened into words. Moreover, she is often not aware that she has rights over her own body.

- If the child thinks that the things that worry her are of little interest to the adults around her, she will believe that nobody will listen to her or take her seriously. She simply does not know how to set about talking about the abuse, nor whom to tell.

- The child remains silent so that she will not hurt her parents. She wishes to avoid telling things which will damage her abuser's reputation, particularly if that person is important to her or highly regarded by those close to her. The child needs to feel accepted and loved, even by the abuser, if he is some-one close whom she cares about. She therefore remains silent so as not to lose that love.

- She is frightened of being scolded or punished, particularly if she has been disobedient or taken undue risks.

- She is ashamed of what has happened, of not having known how to defend herself. She feels guilty – an accessory to the crime. Feeling responsible, she expects to be criticized, misunderstood, and rejected. She may even fear being accused of seducing the perpetrator, or of profiting from the relationship if she has received presents or treats.

- She feels different from others – abnormal in some undefined way.

- She has lost her confidence in the ability of adults to protect her.

- If she has learned that sexual matters are not talked about, she does not dare to ask an adult if the activities she has been involved in are acceptable or not.

- The child is brought up to believe in adult authority, and to conform. This submissiveness is exploited by the abuser, who thus ensures the child's silence. With her lack of experience of the adult world, the child takes the abuser's threats of reprisals literally, believing that they will be carried out if she tells.

As the child grows up, she compares herself with the ideal child portrayed by society. Girls are brought up to please without being provocative. When a girl is abused, she believes that she has led her abuser on and blames herself for not having resisted. She may try to behave as if nothing has happened. Older girls are anxious about having boy-friends, and about future sexual relationships, and this may encourage them to keep silent. Boys want to be brave, resourceful, independent, and capable of looking after themselves. They do not want anyone to know of their helplessness, and will consequently hide the truth.

The child victim of incest

This is more likely to be a girl than a boy. Her loyalties are divided – she loves her father or seducer – and needs his love – while at the same time hating what he does to her. She simultaneously enjoys the privileged relationship and hates the role he makes her play. Often she pities her father, and may hate her mother for not being able to put a stop to the situation. Sometimes she will dissociate herself from the pain and distress, but this may lead to feeling 'cut off' from good and healthy feelings too. Above all, she is afraid of breaking up the family and of being held responsible for the consequences of telling what has happened. She imagines her father arrested, thrown into prison, her family made the subject of gossip. She sees her family deprived of financial support, her mother distraught, herself the object of hate and shame, rejected by her loved ones, and probably sent away from her own home.

Signs of Sexual Abuse

Every case of abuse leaves its mark although the intensity and duration of the hurt may vary. It is therefore vital to recognize the effects of sexual abuse. None of the signs described below should be regarded as concrete proof – most can be attributed to other causes, in particular other forms of ill-treatment. Nevertheless, when faced with one or more of these signs, you should consider sexual abuse a possibility, and investigate further.

Not only parents, but all adults who come into regular contact with children are in a position to pick up these danger signals. It is important to pay attention – these are silent messages from the child's injured body and mind, and she may have no one else in whom she dares to confide.

In the case of incest, where the secret is so closely guarded within the family, recognition and early investigation is the particular responsibility of teachers, school and community nurses, school psychologists, paediatricians, and family doctors.

In some cases, physical signs may suggest or confirm a case of sexual abuse.

The signs are:

- bruises, scratches, burns, or bite marks on the body;

- scratches, abrasions, or persistent infections in the anal or genital regions;

- pregnancy – particularly in the case of young adolescents who are evasive concerning the identity of the father.

More often, the child's behaviour attracts attention. You may notice:

- sexual awareness inappropriate to the child's age: this may be shown in her vocabulary, drawings, or games;
- constant preoccupation with sexual identity;
- frequent masturbation;
- attempts to teach other children about sexual activity;
- sudden and inappropriate modesty, for example refusing to take communal showers at school;
- abdominal pain with no diagnosable cause;
- regressive behaviour such as thumb-sucking, wetting, and soiling;
- clinging behaviour, hanging on to the mother, and refusing to play;
- refusing to stay with certain people or to go to certain places;
- withdrawal from friends, preferring to be alone, running away from home;
- daydreaming, poor school performance, truancy;
- aggressiveness, anger, anxiety, sadness, and tearfulness.

The behaviour may immediately follow the abuse or manifest itself several months later. It may be transitory, lasting from a few days to a few months, or persistent. It all depends on the child, on her situation, and on the help she receives. Some of the signs described above may appear much later, in adolescence or even adulthood, as a result of abuse suffered as a child.

In later life, the following may be significant:

- provocative sexual behaviour, promiscuity, prostitution, sexual abuse of children;
- self-injury, self-destructive behaviour, including alcohol- and drug-abuse, repeated suicide attempts or 'danger-seeking' behaviour;
- emotional difficulties – in particular, problems with personal relationships; over-sensitivity to rejection;

- low self-esteem and lack of self-confidence; self-blame and behaviour which invites exploitation and further physical or sexual abuse.

All of these are avoidable provided that:

- society recognizes the problem of sexual abuse, and the public is made fully aware, starting with the education of children in schools;

- the victim finds a suitable helping agency in whom she can confide;

- that this helping agency believes what the victim says, and reassures her that she is not responsible for the abuse, nor for the consequences of reporting it;

- help is given to avoid a repetition of the abuse and to protect against reprisals;

- the victim is offered specialist therapy if necessary.

6

What to do when the Child Tells her Secret

When the child decides to tell her secret, she may only gradually reveal what has happened to her. She is cautious about what she says, reporting only those facts which are least upsetting to her, or expressing herself indirectly or imprecisely. She may hold back the whole truth if she is not sure of the reliability of her confidant. Her attempt to confide therefore risks going unnoticed, or not being taken sufficiently seriously.

It is important to remember that children rarely lie. How could she have learnt of these sexual activities if not by being involved? If she retracts, and says that she has been lying, it may be because she is being pressurized by an adult, or is trying to spare someone she loves.

The child has been brave to break her silence. She wants to understand why she has suffered, and hopes that it is at an end, but is afraid that no one will believe her, or that she will be punished. She needs above all to find a sympathetic ear and to be reassured that she was right to tell. She should be made to feel that she is loved as much as ever, and that she will receive help.

What to do straight away:

● choose somewhere quiet, where the child feels safe to talk to you in private;

● listen carefully to the child – encourage her to tell what she remembers, and agree with her that some things are painful and difficult to talk about;

● take her at her word. If need be, help her to be more specific on certain points;

● thank her for confiding in you. Reassure her that she has done well to talk to you, and that she is neither responsible for the abuse, not for its consequences, even if she has been disobedient or taken unnecessary risks;

● tell her that the abuser had no right to do what he did – it is forbidden by law – and that the abuser should be punished for what he has done, although he is not necessarily a bad or wicked person;

● promise her that you will support her. Tell her that you will take steps to put a stop to the situation and get help, and that you are able to do this.

Do not:

● let other people interrupt or become involved unnecessarily;

● over-dramatize the situation, punish, or criticize the child;

● confront the child with the abuser. The child is frightened of being called a liar and of reprisals;

● criticize the child for not having spoken earlier, or for allowing the abuse to happen;

● promise the child to keep her secret: other people will have to be told;

● try to force her to forget what happened.

Then:

- carry on listening to the child without showing irritation even if she repeats herself. Let her take her own time to tell you in her own way;

- show respect for her disclosure by not gossiping with those not involved. If you do, the child may be teased or rejected by those around her;

- encourage her to resume or to take up interests which will give her positive experiences and help her to make friends – at the same time, do not push her beyond her capacity;

- praise her positive qualities and abilities, and encourage her capacity for creativity.

7

Methods of Intervention

- What do you do, and whom do you tell when you know that a child has been sexually abused by a stranger?

- What do you do when a victim of incest has confided in you?

- What do you do when, having noticed the signs in a child you know well, you strongly suspect that she is being mistreated or sexually abused within her family circle?

- What do you do if you yourself are a young victim?

What steps do you take? Whom do you contact to get help and to put a stop to the situation? What risks does a person run who takes it upon himself to intervene? And what if, having heard an abused child's disclosure, you do nothing?

In considering how to answer all these questions, the welfare of the child must be paramount.

The need to inform

There is no legal obligation to report suspicion of child abuse. It is nevertheless the clear moral duty of all those concerned with child welfare to do so.

The man or woman in the street can invent a thousand reasons for not reporting their suspicions or knowledge.

- There may be lack of understanding about the frequency or seriousness of such activity. Frank disbelief alone may make them keep silent.

- There may be fear of 'telling tales' about a person of good reputation, someone whom they like, or to whom they are close.

- There may be fear of reprisals, even violence, from the abuser towards the victim, or towards the informer, or of the abuser committing suicide.

- There may be fear that the child and his family may be rejected and ostracized by neighbours and friends.

- There may be fear of a prison sentence for the abuser, with loss of financial support for his wife and children.

- There may be fear of 'getting involved', even having to make a statement to the police, or worse still, having to give evidence in court.

In deciding how to act, it must be remembered that these issues do not depend solely on the confidant's own conscience or on the competence of any one professional body.

Children have a right to be protected by the law – legislation exists in the form of the Children and Young Persons Act 1933, the Children and Young Persons Act 1969, the Child Care Act 1980, and, from October 1991, the Children Act 1989. Child abuse is also indictable under the Sexual Offences Act 1965, and the Offences Against the Person Act 1861. These statutes embody provision for proper protection of the child in any situation where there is real or suspected abuse. Each district has its own Social Services organization, with a team of specially trained social workers who are experienced in matters concerning child protection and can take the necessary steps for the child's welfare. *See* Appendix 2.

Tell the professionals

Fear of the police and legal machinery could prompt someone to take the law into his or her own hands, and to try to resolve the problem instead of alerting the authorities.

This may well make the situation worse, and opens the individual to the possibility of a slander action at least, and at worst violence. In the absence of an effective means of helping the victim, the child may suffer even more.

It is important to remember that an abused child who gets to the point of admitting what has happened and does not then receive support may well retract her admission, and take refuge in yet further silence and isolation.

In reporting the case without delay you are:

● proving to the victim that you believe her;

● protecting not only her, but maybe other members of her family or peer group;

● helping the victim to get the support and counselling she needs;

● helping the police to find a criminal;

● giving the abuser the opportunity to receive help.

If you are uncertain, just remind yourself that it is the abuser who caused the problem, not the informer, nor the child.

The child's feelings must always be taken into account before embarking on any course of action. The reasons for the various steps and decisions to be taken should always be explained to her, and her co-operation should be sought at each stage of the proceedings. This will help her to regain a feeling of control and restore her damaged self-respect.

She should repeatedly be told that children can never be responsible for the abuse.

The protection of the child is paramount in all cases. She should be asked what would make her feel safe – what sort of protection would she like? She can be removed from her home to ensure this, but it is often better for the victim to be able to stay in her own familiar surroundings. Where the abuser lives in the same house, he can be offered other accommodation in order to be able to leave.

Whom to inform?

Both the police and social workers have the authority to investigate and to institute procedures to protect the child under the Children Act 1989.

All Social Services departments have an Area Child Protection Committee (ACPC), on which all relevant agencies are represented at a senior level. The District Health Authority should also agree policies and procedures regarding child welfare, and these should be formulated in writing to complement the policy of the ACPC.

All doctors have access to these written policies and should be familiar with them so that they will know how to act if the child confides in them. Further guidance is available in the DHSS Guidelines *Child Abuse: Working Together* and in *Diagnosis of Child Sexual Abuse: Guidance for Doctors* (*see* Resources).

Contact may also be made with voluntary organizations such as the NSPCC.

Following the initial contact, the best possible intervention is by a co-ordinated team of experienced professionals. Each member of the team should have a clearly defined role to play, and the planned procedure should be clear, rapid, intensive, and well co-ordinated.

In general, Social Services are responsible for bringing together the appropriate professionals, who can together draw up a plan of action to support the child and her parents. They will then go on to co-ordinate the rehabilitation procedure for the family. This will involve practical measures including accommodation and financial support, together with therapy for the victim, often for the family as a whole, and, wherever possible, for the perpetrator.

Intervention may also involve the police in preferring criminal charges against the abuser, and the medical profession in undertaking an appropriate medico-legal examination of the victim.

In all cases, the first step for the victim is the same — she must speak to someone in authority whom she trusts, and who can institute the appropriate action on her behalf.

The first step for the individual who has been informed or is suspicious is also the same — to pass the information to a responsible authority who has the power to intervene on behalf of the child's welfare.

What to do in different cases

1. Sexual abuse by a stranger.

2. Abuse within the family.

In both cases, three objectives should be borne in mind.

● You should listen carefully to the abused child and help her to obtain the support she needs.

● You should protect the victim and put an immediate stop to the abuse.

● You should introduce secondary preventive measures with the aim of preventing a recurrence. These may include education of the child, her family, and others in the neighbourhood, counselling and therapy for those involved, and possibly legal proceedings leading to conviction and rehabilitation for the offender.

Abuse by a stranger

Help for the victim

You should be educated, observant, and aware. Even if the child does not tell anyone what has happened, it may often be deduced from changes in her behaviour. The person who notices this should try to persuade the child to confide. Many children have remained silent because no one has actually asked them directly about abuse.

When she does talk about it, the fact that someone really listens is already therapeutic.

When her mother is not the person in whom she confides, she or both the child's parents must be told as soon as possible.

In general, a child who is listened to, believed, and reassured, who sees that she is important to her parents, will be able to tell them fully about her experiences. She will gradually feel comforted and begin to get back to normal. If the distress is persistent or severe, then specialist help should be sought. Adolescents in particular often need a broader framework than that of their immediate family.

Many children who have been abused have fears and anxieties about their bodies and their physical health. A sensitive and well-conducted medical examination will help to reassure them that no permanent damage has been done.

Psychotherapy consists primarily of allowing the victim to talk about her traumatic experiences. The most important step is to establish trust in the therapist, and the child will then be able to express her unease, her ambivalence, and her fears, perhaps through the media of play or drawing.

Help for the parents

Not all parents feel capable of coping with such situations, or of responding to the child's needs. Many of the questions the child asks can be distressing, and her reactions unexpected. Even the most caring parents can feel out of their depth. It is important that they themselves receive professional help in order to support the child better. They may also be helped in being able to discuss appropriate steps to take with regard to the abuser.

Protecting the victim and suppressing the abuse

The circumstances of the abuse must be considered.

● Does the child know her abuser?

● Is he someone she cannot avoid meeting in her everyday life?

● Is the abuser someone involved with her school, her leisure activities, or her family life within the home?

● Is he an adult, an older child, or a relative?

The child should always be asked what would make her feel safe – what kind of protection does she feel that she needs? She may prefer to have time off school, or to be accompanied on her way there. She may wish to change her leisure activities, and have some advice about how best to defend herself.

The questioning of the victim takes place after due thought and planning by a multidisciplinary team, and with the minimum of delay. It should be carried out by specially trained social workers or police officers who have had experience of this kind of work. For further information about interviewing procedures *see* Chapter 8.

Preventing a repetition of the offence

Other children who may be thought to be at risk should be provided with appropriate information in a non-frightening way. This can be done at school by those responsible for the sex education programme, by members of a voluntary organization, or in the home by parents themselves.

Parents must always be educated about the detection of child sexual abuse, and the appropriate procedure to follow if they are suspicious.

Police or social work investigations need to progress at least as far as confronting the individual with the offence and its consequences. Charges may or may not be preferred, depending on an assessment of the situation, and the willingness of the abuser to enter into therapy.

However, conviction and sentencing of the perpetrator means that he is obliged to accept that he alone is responsible for the acts and their consequences. This may be a necessary part of his rehabilitation.

Nevertheless, conviction and punishment do not always rule out the danger of repetition. They should be accompanied by appropriate treatment aimed at altering the abuser's behaviour. This can take place during his detention, or while he is on parole.

Now that it is known that many adult sex offenders began their activities in adolescence, it cannot be emphasized too strongly how important this kind of help is for the younger abuser, whose pattern of behaviour may be more amenable to change. He can be helped to distinguish his need for contact, tenderness, and friendship from his sexual desires, and to recognize his violence as an expression of fear of rejection.

Sexual abuse within the family

In this case, protection of the victim and stopping the abuse are the main priorities.

In many cases of incest, the child victim runs away from home in order to protect herself, only to find that her inexperience, precarious circumstances, and previous trauma make her vulnerable to fresh abuse from others.

It is an ideal but rare situation in which the family itself recognizes its need for help, and seeks it from the appropriate authorities.

More often, incest is revealed by adolescent victims when their mental health is affected, or by courageous mothers who assume the responsibility of protecting their children. The reception that the informant receives at this point is crucial to the outcome.

Sadly, it is often as part of divorce or separation proceedings that these facts come to light, and this can accentuate the child's feelings of guilt and responsibility for the break-up of the family. At this stage, psychological intervention is often regarded as an intrusion, and it is impossible to restore more normal relationships within the family.

Sexual abuse, like physical abuse, is committed in secret, and in a situation of social and emotional isolation. This means that the abuse may escalate, and that the chances of spontaneous improvement are slight. Repetition increases the abuser's feelings of failure as a parent, producing inner conflict and despair. The child is unable to distance herself from, or give up her affection for the abuser. She accepts the unacceptable, blames herself, and tells no-one. Her suffering, confusion and isolation may translate into abnormal behaviour as a cry for help.

Those who hear and respond to this cry for help are acting as much in the interests of the parents as of the child. They should be fully aware of the fact that the crisis they are precipitating is an essential part of true and lasting change within the family, and the beginning of a return to health for the family members.

Whom to tell?
It is certainly possible to seek advice anonymously through the various voluntary organizations offering telephone counselling and advice. However, only Social Services and the police are able to take urgent action to protect the child.

To safeguard the security of the victim, it is important that the action taken should be authoritative, competent, and co-ordinated. Firmness and clarity are needed to counter the abuser's threats: an understanding but firm approach will show him that there are other methods of expression than abusive behaviour and violence. Nevertheless, a violent response to the accusation is always possible, and it may be necessary for the police to act in such cases.

The abuser and the victim should be separated immediately, and the abuser rather than the child should leave the family home. Social Services are sometimes able to provide financial support for this move if necessary. If the child is removed from her family and familiar environment, she will feel that she is being punished, and this will increase her sense of guilt. The mother/child relationship is very important in the eventual recovery of the victim, and this should be preserved at all costs.

Confidentiality is essential – for the victim in order to be able to confide fully, and for the abuser in helping him to admit his responsibility.

It is also important for the child to know that the abuser is not just going to be punished, but will also receive help.

Psychotherapy will be a vital part of the treatment.

For the family as a group:

● to bring about and to sustain changes in the interaction between family members;

● to re-establish demarcation lines between generations and to restore 'personal space' for each individual;

● to improve open communication both within the family, and between the family and the outside world.

For the child:

● to help her recover from the trauma she has suffered, and to make a new start;

● to learn to recognize and to express her emotional and practical needs;

- to rebuild her personal and sexual identity, learning to distinguish affection from sexual behaviour;
- to give her a clear idea of the protective and caring role of normal healthy parents;
- to learn to emerge from her isolation and to resume her proper role as a child, renewing her relationship with her brothers and sisters, and learning again how to play with her peer group;
- by discovering, or re-discovering, a stable and trusting relationship with an adult.

For her brothers and sisters:

- to provide the necessary help for their emotional involvement in a disturbed family.

For the mother:

- to make the time to listen and to understand;
- to learn or to consolidate her maternal role: to care for her children by offering a tender and protective environment of which she herself may have been deprived as a child;
- to allow her to become independent in a gradual and comfortable way.

For the couple:

- to recognize their personal problems, particularly those related to sex and emotion, and to discuss strategies for working at them together without involving the children;
- by letting each other decide on the necessary steps to take (in particular in cases of alcohol abuse) and to follow them either individually or together.

For the abusing parent:

- to recognize his full responsibility for the abuse and the manipulation to which he has subjected his victim;
- to understand the suffering that he has inflicted;
- to master his abusive impulses and to rehabilitate him in the role of father, capable of providing protection and guidance to his children.

Three-way therapy

Experience both in Canada and in California has shown that an integrated therapeutic approach can be most effective in dealing with families of incest victims. This 'three-way therapy' involves all members of the family in therapy sessions, while the abusing parent also receives individual therapy and treatment in a group with other abusing fathers. The fathers, who often at first deny what they have done, are brought into contact with others who have committed incest in the past. They can therefore be helped to accept responsibility and treatment. These groups put an end to the isolation of incestuous families and give rise to a feeling of togetherness and hope for the future.

Experience of this kind of therapy has shown that the father can change with the help and support of his wife and family, knowing that they still care for him in spite of what he has done. Even if the wife does eventually feel that divorce is the only possible option, she comes to her decision as the result of proper consideration, rather than in the heat of the moment at disclosure.

The fact that mothers and children come together in groups for mutual support reduces the risk of repetition once the family is reunited.

8

The Investigation

Interviewing the child

The questioning of the victim takes place after due thought and planning by the multidisciplinary team, and with the minimum of delay. It should normally be carried out by social workers or police who have had training and experience in interviewing children of different ages.

The purpose of the interview is not only to obtain facts — it will also need to reassure the child and her carers that the matter is being taken seriously and will be handled in a sensitive way.

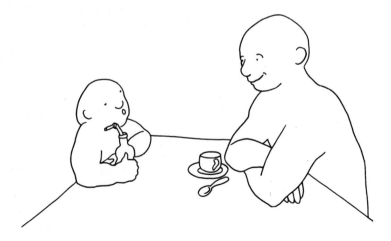

It should take place in a setting where the child feels comfortable – in her own home, or perhaps that of a trusted relative or friend. Some police authorities have special interview suites, furnished and decorated in a homely manner, where a relaxed atmosphere can be created on neutral ground.

All information obtained should be carefully recorded. A video tape of the interview may prevent the child having to be re-interviewed at a later stage. This may be admissible in court if the case comes to prosecution.

The medical examination

All serious allegations of aggression or abuse necessitating a medical examination put the doctor in a difficult position, involving unusual ethical, technical, and legal factors.

Children not only have feelings of insecurity, guilt, and anger, but also fears about their bodily integrity. Adolescents are often frightened of pregnancy or of sexually transmitted disease; may be concerned about their future fertility and sexuality or even simply about the appearance of their sexual organs.

A full examination, implemented with tact and care, should be carried out as soon as possible. This should not be limited just to establishing the facts or excluding infection or pregnancy – it represents a privileged opportunity to reassure the anxious child with regard to her physical health both now and in the future.

The child's consent to the examination is important. For consent to be valid it must be informed (i.e. the child must be aware of what she is consenting to and the possible consequences), and freely given, without fear, deception, or coercion. Written consent is preferable. Children over 16 are regarded in law as capable of giving consent, but can also refuse it if given by an adult on their behalf. Younger children may also be regarded as capable of giving consent, depending on their age or understanding. For children who are not regarded as capable of giving consent, formal consent must be sought from a parent or those with parental rights.

Professional confidentiality is a difficult issue for doctors. However, when a matter of serious crime is involved, it is not only permissible for the doctor to disclose relevant information to a third party, but also his duty to do so. The doctor owes a duty of confidentiality both to the parent and to the child, but where these duties conflict, the welfare of the child should be paramount. Guidance is given in *Diagnosis of Child Sexual Abuse: Guidance for Doctors* (*see* Resources) and can also be obtained from any of the medical defence societies.

For the initial examination, the doctor's duty will be to take a careful social and medical history, including any current symptoms, and a general examination, making full notes of all findings. If the history and circumstances suggest sexual abuse, the doctor may wish to arrange a fuller examination by a suitably trained paediatrician or police surgeon.

This should take place in a suitably private room with adequate facilities for screening for sexually transmitted disease, and the collection of forensic specimens. It is recommended that the doctor should use a sexual offences kit, available from police or forensic laboratories. Clinical photography may also be used.

Throughout the examination, the child should be reassured, and the necessary procedures should be explained carefully to her. Thorough and complete records should be made at all stages, together with notes of any comments made by the child during the examination.

9

Education and Prevention of Sexual Abuse

Three principles are important here:

● respect for the individual;

● the recognition of the rights of the child;

● a clear understanding of the responsibility of adults of different disciplines with regard to children.

In safeguarding the security of children and helping them to recognize and to resist attempted abuse, prevention also aims to:

● dispel ignorance and alert people to the frequency and potential dangers of sexual abuse by providing information targeted at specific groups, e.g. parents, children, teachers, doctors and social workers;

● improve the awareness of parents and increase their ability to protect their children;

● develop in children a sense of their personal rights and freedoms, teaching them discrimination and an ability to set limits, the capacity to protect themselves and to seek appropriate help, and encouraging them to talk openly to trusted adults.

Prevention is a shared responsibility, and should become a priority for all authorities involved in child care. Multiple and well co-ordinated strategies should be evolved by both statutory and voluntary bodies with the aim of:

● providing information for families and the general public;

- making teachers and others involved with children properly aware;
- establishing special educational programmes for children and adolescents;
- ensuring further training for the professionals concerned with recognition and treatment.

Primary prevention comprises global prevention and specific prevention.

Global prevention

This is concerned with education about relationships and parenting in general, and within the family in particular. Parents play the principal preventive role as educators of their children, and in their ability to protect their children. The ability to be a good parent does not simply arrive with the baby at birth – most parents have learnt their roles from their own parents and experience of their own childhood.

It is well recognized that the prospect of becoming parents awakens anxieties in a young couple. They will need companionship and counselling to combat the social isolation which often follows the arrival of a new baby.

They will need to learn how to respond to the physical and emotional demands of the baby without rejecting their partner, and how to sustain the strengths of the marital relationship while preserving some individuality within it. Parents can and should be taught how to create a strong, stable bond with their infant, and still be able to respect her individuality.

These strong, stable bonds are created from the very beginning of a baby's life. They satisfy the baby's need for human contact, and, in turn, teach her to be able to create new bonds for herself, making friends and relationships with others in later life.

It is in providing this early care that the parent assumes a protective role. It follows that a father who shares in this care from the beginning establishes a close relationship with the baby, and is able to take on the role of protector. This alone diminishes the risk of later incest.

The creation of a strong and independent personality in the child and the development of a healthy adult sexuality demands the ability of the child to separate herself from the parent. The ability to tolerate separation develops soon after birth, and the child who is confident of her parents' love is able to separate without undue anxiety.

Parents should be educated to develop a better understanding of their child, and to be able to seek appropriate help and advice if difficulties arise. This education can be provided in the school, in parentcraft classes during the pregnancy, in day centres for parents and children, and in a multitude of other settings. The attitude of teachers, doctors, health visitors, and other professionals involved in child care will also provide a useful model.

Specific prevention

As well as education on sexual matters within the family, school plays an invaluable complementary role. Specific information can be provided within classes on sex education or sociology, so that it can reach all children, even those whose families are not able to discuss these matters at home.

Sex education within the school should be adapted according to the age of the child, and presented in a sensitive way. It should confirm the child's rights as an individual by reinforcing the need for discrimination, her self-esteem, and her ability to find appropriate help if necessary. Better understanding of her own body and her emotions will lead to the development of a healthy sexuality which can evolve through to adulthood. It will explain what is normal and acceptable, and what is not.

Children are not generally disturbed by what they are taught about sexual abuse if they are reminded that they have the right to reject approaches, and will be supported if they do so. This kind of teaching should be part of a general education about the risks and dangers they may encounter in life, and they should be taught how to protect themselves.

Professionals who come into contact with children should familiarize themselves with recent developments in the field of research and investigation into child sexual abuse.

In order to be more receptive to children, parents and teachers must be more open themselves, rejecting myths and prejudices. If adults are able to discuss these subjects with ease, and know how to facilitate discussions with children, they will be regarded as approachable for further information and help. They must listen carefully to what children have to say and learn how to identify child abuse when it occurs.

What should a parent tell children?

Here are seven key points which may be useful.

1. Your body belongs to you, your mind and your thoughts belong to you – and to no one else.

2. You have the same right to respect as everyone else.

3. You have the right to say no, to impose limits, to refuse whatever displeases you.

4. Trust in your intuition. You have the right to protect yourself and to ask for help.

5. Use your critical sense in situations you meet. Think about what you believe, choose people whom you trust – you have the right to do so.

6. There is no absolute secret which you cannot share with people you trust. Tell someone what has happened to you. You have the right to talk about what is on your mind.

7. Make good friends on whom you can rely.

These key points can help to reduce the risk of aggression and abuse. Adults must, however, show that they really believe in these principles by adopting them in their own lives.

Parents should nevertheless remember that:

● the younger the child, the more she depends on her parents to protect her;

- even the most well-informed child, however independent and able to protect herself, cannot be totally safe;

- even parents who are fully aware of the potential dangers can be deceived.

Neither the trapped child nor the deceived parent should allow their feelings of incompetence and guilt to stand in the way of obtaining help and putting a stop to the abuse.

Respecting the child and the development of her sexuality

The young child needs to establish a close bodily contact with her carer. This does not, however, mean possession – it is important that the parent acknowledges the child's individuality, and can develop closeness together with respect for her separateness.

The child's sexuality develops in the light of her own sensory experiences. In discovering the world around her through her senses, she experiences both pleasure and pain. Amongst her first discoveries are the different parts of her own body – her hands, her feet, her genital organs.

Often when a child plays with her genital organs, she experiences a simple pleasure, free from moral implications. She should be allowed to do this naturally without criticism or punishment.

When she begins to talk, she learns the names of the different parts of her body. She should be taught the proper names for her genital organs and understand that she has a right to recognize and know them.

Most children who live in a trusting environment like to be naked, and to see others the same. Playing 'doctors and nurses' for example, is a game of discovery which helps them to establish their own sexual identity.

If she has learned to recognize, respect, and care for her own genital organs, she will be able to demand that others respect them too, and will be better able to protect herself. If she has seen the naked bodies of other children and adults within her own family as part of normal behaviour, she will more easily identify an abuser's behaviour as abnormal.

Parents should understand that the best basis for the developing child's personality and confidence is love. Physical contact and caresses are important in the communication of this love. They should also remember that sexuality is like a flower – at first a bud, it opens from within, at its own pace. Any attempt to hasten its blossoming may compromise its healthy development.

The curiosity of children regarding sexual matters should not be mistaken for sexual needs in the adult sense. Adult, genital sexuality is determined by hormonal changes at puberty. Pre-pubertal children do not have sexual needs, but may borrow the language of adults to express their feelings of love and affection. They should be taught appropriate words of tenderness and other ways of showing their love.

The child's right to say no

As adults, we react to people and events with varying degrees of pleasure, sadness, fear, and with feelings of love and under-standing. Even a very small child has surprisingly strong feelings of this kind. We should not dictate to her what she should feel. She has the right to discriminate, and to choose whether to be involved with someone or not. For example, there is nothing to be achieved by making a child kiss a relative she does not like. By teaching her to be nice to everyone, we are making her more vulnerable.

We should trust her, and teach her that she has rights to her personal feelings and personal space. If she learns to say no in this kind of situation, she will find it easier to do so when adults behave in an ambiguous way.

Respecting the boundaries

Respect for the child is only part of a general respect of boundaries between the generations. However close one is to one's child or parents, however much one can confide in them, there is always a boundary, and this provides part of the stable framework of the family.

It is the close and strong relationship between the parents which provides a firm structure within which the child can develop and become independent.

When adults show that they are in control of their sexual feelings, the adolescent can safely seek appreciation from the parents for their own physical attractiveness and masculine or feminine development.

When a child finds that a parent does not allow the sexualization of the relationship, her sexual feelings are appropriately turned towards her own generation.

It is obviously more difficult to maintain this structure within a one-parent family. The child may drift into the role of the missing parent, and boundaries may become blurred.

Clarifying the boundary between tenderness and abuse

How do you distinguish the healthy bodily contact which gives the child her sense of security and strength from that which exploits her and risks hindering her development. Where is the demarcation between normal touching and inappropriate sexual behaviour? When does parental tenderness go beyond soothing contact and become a seduction which takes the child beyond her real needs − a possessive love which makes undue demands on her?

As an adult, one can judge the point at which the boundary has been crossed by the embarrassment felt when such behaviour is observed. When there is a need to pretend, the behaviour has become too erotic. Even small children know very well when the contact has gone too far − they turn away, try to get free, fight, or cry. This is the way they show that their limits have been reached, and their need for physical contact is satisfied.

The adult who exceeds the limits satisfies his own needs at the expense of the child, using his power and authority to do so. This is the point at which abuse begins.

Developing intuition and common sense

Everyone has an internal sense which alerts them to uncomfortable situations. This intuitive sense is often particularly well developed in children, and they should be given the chance to use it. Encourage it by asking them how they feel about certain events and people, and by expressing your own intuition in a similar way.

Common sense develops with experience. Children gradually discover the dark side of life – pain, sadness, and failure as well as unhappiness, wickedness, and lack of understanding. They need to talk about these aspects and to try to understand them. Encourage them to be critical, to have opinions, and to discuss how they would have reacted in a similar situation. Teach them that not all the information they see or hear in the media is accurate or even acceptable. Your own opinions will be a useful bench-mark for them.

Self-reliance

Small children are often distressed by their feelings of dependence and helplessness. As they grow older, their daily experiences help them to discover their own ability to control their environment. By exercising their freedom of choice, they develop self-confidence. As far as possible, children should be allowed to make decisions which directly concern them, and to be aware of their needs and personal preferences. For example, they should be free to choose their own friends, what to spend their pocket-money on, what sport to take up, and even which subjects to study.

When a child wants to have a go at doing something which seems to be too hard for her, let her try. Help her by discussing beforehand some of the problems she may encounter. She will learn from both her achievements and her failures, and will be able to translate her helplessness into a degree of control. Parents may prevent children from attempting difficult tasks for their own sake – because it is too painful to see their child fail.

Trust

A child naturally trusts her parents, but to be able to confide in them she needs to feel that they really want to listen and are concerned. If she feels that she matters to them and that they take her worries seriously, she will be able to tell them about any abusive situation she may meet.

What makes adults approachable is their availability. They need to set aside time to listen and to try to understand.

Open communication about sexual matters is also important – the child will know that her parents are being honest with her and, in turn, will be able to tell them about any sexual matters that have upset her.

There should be open discussion about different ways of touching or caressing. Children should be asked which kinds of touching make them happy, uneasy, or frightened.

Children have a natural trust in people they know. It is important to explain to them that although most people love children, there are some who, because of their own problems, can be harmful to them. Avoid categorizing people as good and bad – this will give them the idea that only 'nasty' people would harm them, and will leave them defenceless against the seductive abuser.

A child's natural sense of justice is shaken if she finds that adults and children are judged by different standards.

Communication and secrets

Speech and language are important aspects of the development of the child. It is through speech that she will learn about the world around her, and develop friendships and the ability to share experiences with others.

The articulate child can also use speech to distance people she does not like, to keep the abuser at bay, or at least to gain valuable time. It is also necessary in seeking help. It can be useful in explaining the difference between 'telling tales' and asking for help when she feels threatened.

We should teach children to value and to master effective communication. It contributes both to their development and to their protection – an important preventive measure.

Secrets create a state of isolation, which can be dangerous. Good secrets are those which bring happiness – for example, a surprise birthday present. Bad secrets are those which feel uncomfortable or frightening. Children should never keep kisses, cuddles, or hugs a secret.

The rule never to keep a bad secret to oneself has a very real preventive value. Some abusers set out by seeing how well the child can keep a secret. If the child knows that only surprises are good secrets, she will refuse to take part in something she is forbidden to tell about.

Friendships

The quality of the relationship between friends is particularly precious. The pleasure of shared interests, activities, discussions and the mutual exchange of ideas is part of the child's development, and enriches her life beyond the family circle.

Furthermore, the company of other children is a useful safety factor.

- As a group, children are in a better position to protect themselves.
- Abusers are more likely to pick out a child on her own.
- A sociable child runs less risk of being entangled in a destructive relationship.

Encouraging the child to have friends of her own age is therefore an important preventive measure. Help her to join in group activities and outings, and make her friends welcome in your home. Be ready to comfort the child who finds it difficult to make friends, and praise her courage in trying to do so. Be sympathetic to the child who feels let down by a friend's actions, and help her to talk out the problems within the relationship. She will learn that friendships can be all the stronger if she can persevere when things go wrong.

APPENDIX 1

Practical Advice

Advice for parents and teachers

- Do not let small children play unsupervised in the street or in public places. Do not let them go off on their own to isolated areas. Always accompany them to public lavatories.

- Teach your child at the earliest opportunity her name, address, and telephone number.

- Talk to your child about the professionals she can trust when, for example, she has to ask the way. Explain to her where she is allowed to go and where she is not.

- Be clear about safety measures – tell her not to stay in the park when her friends have gone home, not to play in the street after dark.

- Do not load her with too many rules all at once. Choose rules which apply particularly to her and her life-style.

- Discuss examples of unfamiliar situations – What would you do if . . .?

- Tell her that you really want to know if anything unpleasant happens to her, and reassure her that you would be able to help.

- When you go out with her to a crowded place, pick out a person she could safely approach if she were lost. Agree on a well-lit and safe place to meet if you get separated.

- Make sure your child knows her way home from school, from the park, from her friend's house. Familiarize yourself with the route. Encourage her to stay with a group of friends, and not to wander off on her own.

- Teach her always to be punctual. If you are always on time, and always let her know where you are going, she will learn to do the same.

- Make sure she lets you know if she is visiting a friend, and agree a suitable time for her to come home.

- Get to know the names, addresses, and telephone numbers of her friends. Make a point of noticing the adults your child knows. Be wary of those who seem over-attentive or over-generous.

- In the case of an older child, get to know her circle of friends, where they meet, and how they get there. Consider collecting her or paying for her to come home by taxi if she is going to be late.

- If for any reason, your child is late coming home, do not panic! Stay calm, telephone the places she might be, and notify the police. Use a neighbour's telephone so that your line will stay free in case she should ring.

Remember:

- Children are never to blame for having been abused.

- Parents are not to blame if their child is abused – even if they have failed to protect her, they did the best they could.

- The one to blame is the person who chooses to sexually abuse a child. There is no excuse.

Advice for adolescents

People of this age often feel invulnerable. They also have a need to be 'one of a group' and may resent the parent for making them feel different by keeping to safety rules. It is important to discuss with them the risks they wish to take.

Key points that may be useful for them:

- respect yourself and others;

- take note of your intuition and act on it, even if it makes you feel silly, naïve, or impolite;

- keep to what you feel is right and safe, not necessarily following what the others in the group do.

Rules for children

Be alert in every new situation. To know if it is dangerous, ask yourself these three questions:

- does the answer feel like a yes or a no inside?

- am I sure that I can find help – someone I can trust or a place that feels safe – if I need to?

● do my parents know how to find me – and could they, if things go wrong?

If you reply yes three times, you can go. If even only one answer is no, do *not* go. Go back to someone you can trust.

Safety in public

● Do not trust a stranger who starts talking to you.

● If someone stops you to ask you the way, show him (or tell him you do not know), but never go with him.

● If a stranger asks you for help, tell him to ask an adult.

● Never go anywhere with a stranger, even to a party, and do not let him bring you home.

● Never accept a present from a stranger or a friend if you do not understand why it was given.

● If someone approaches you when you are alone in the family car, sound the horn.

● Stay together as a group in the street or in public places. After dark, choose well-lit and busy streets. Do not take short cuts through alley-ways or across open ground.

● Know how to reverse the charges on a telephone if you do not have money. Remember 999 calls to the police are free.

● If you are lost and need directions, ask a policeman or a sales woman in a shop.

● Never give your name and address to a stranger, nor any information about your family.

● Never accept lifts in a car.

● If someone does threaten you, try to attract attention: shout, throw something, kick, bite, run away. If you are followed, run towards people.

● If anything does happen to you, or one of your friends, tell your parents, your teacher, or the police straight away.

APPENDIX 2

Legal Aspects of Protection of the Abused Child

The actions that can be taken when child sexual abuse is suspected or confirmed fall into four main categories.

The first relates to the protection of the child under the Child Care Act 1980 (from October 1991, the Children Act 1989).

In some cases it is appropriate for the child to take civil action against the abuser in order to prevent further abuse or to claim damages.

Thirdly, there may be financial redress for the child through the Criminal Injuries Compensation procedure.

Lastly, there can, of course, be prosecution of the offender under existing criminal law.

The Child Care Act 1980 and the Children Act 1989

Under the old Child Care Act 1980 there is a duty of the local authority to receive into care a child placed there voluntarily by its parents. Under Section 3, the authority can compulsorily retain care of a child originally placed under a voluntary arrangement.

If care is not voluntarily sought by the parents, but seems to be in the child's best interest, the authority has to enter care proceedings under the Children and Young Persons Act 1969. It can alternatively seek a Care and Control Order after wardship proceedings in the High Court. Courts also have jurisdiction in certain family proceedings to commit a child to care if it seems appropriate. This could be in divorce or other proceedings, such as those related to guardianship or adoption.

To get a Compulsory Care Order either under Section 3 of the 1980 Act or the 1969 Act, the local authority has to show that a child's unsatisfactory situation arose from abuse or neglect, exposure to moral danger, delinquency, or being beyond parental control.

The new Children Act 1989 is due to come into force in October 1991. The implications of this new Act, and the ways in which it will be implemented by lawyers and social workers are not yet entirely clear. The stated ethos of the new Act is to ensure that the child's welfare is the paramount consideration, and there is new emphasis on taking into account the child's own wishes and feelings, considered in the light of her age and understanding.

The sections of the new Act relevant to child sexual abuse are mainly contained in Parts IV and V which relate to the protection of children.

The actions which can be taken include:

A Child Assessment Order (Part V, Section 43)

The court may make such an order on the application of a local authority or that of another authorized person if it is satisfied that:

- the applicant has reasonable cause to believe that the child is suffering or is likely to suffer significant harm;
- an assessment is needed to determine whether such harm has been or is likely to be suffered;
- it is unlikely that such an assessment will be made in the absence of such an order.

The order specifies the date on which the assessment begins, and lasts for a maximum of seven days.

The child and its parents or guardians should be informed before the hearing of the application.

An Emergency Child Assessment Order (Part V, Section 44)

This order gives the applicant parental responsibility for the child. The order can be made by the court on the application of a local authority or other authorized person, e.g. parent, guardian, NSPCC officer, if it is satisfied that:

- there is reasonable cause to believe that the child is likely to suffer significant harm if she is not removed to, or does not stay in, care or other safe accommodation;

- further enquiries are being made under Section 47(1)(b) with respect to the child's welfare;

- those enquiries are being frustrated by access to the child being unreasonably refused.

This order is effective for not more than eight days, but can be extended by a further seven days on one occasion only. After 72 hours, the child, her parent, or her guardian may apply for the order to be discharged.

If the child is of sufficient understanding to make an informed decision, she is entitled to consent or refuse to submit to a medical and/or a psychiatric examination (Section 44.7).

Action by the police (Part V, Section 46)

Any police officer who has reason to believe that the child may otherwise be harmed:

- may remove the child to suitable accommodation;

● should also inform the parents or guardian of the child of the action and the reasons for it; inform the local authority, and ensure that the case is enquired into by a designated police officer.

This police protection lasts for only 72 hours, during which time an emergency protection order application can be made.

Care and Supervision Orders (Part IV, Section 31)

On the application of any local authority or other authorized person, the court may make an order:

● placing the child in the care of a designated local authority (Care Order); or;

● placing her under the supervision of a designated local authority or probation officer (Supervision Order).

The court may only make the Care or Supervision Order if:

● the child is suffering or is likely to suffer significant harm; and

● the harm or likelihood of it is attributable to the care given the child being 'less than it would be reasonable to expect a parent to give'.

Where a Care Order is made, it is the duty of the local authority designated in the Order to receive the child into care, and to assume parental responsibility. The authority may appoint a guardian for the child. A Care Order may be discharged on the application of the child herself, her parent or guardian, or the local authority.

A Supervision Order may require the child to undergo medical or psychiatric examination, provided that, if the child has sufficient understanding to make an informed decision, she consents to be examined. The court is also empowered to order the child to attend all or part of the proceedings. Supervision Orders last a year.

The court may use its discretion in making either a Care or Supervision Order, irrespective of the type of application submitted. Either of these Orders may alternatively be made as interim Orders for a specified length of time or until other arrangements can be made.

NB Section 100 (2) of the Children Act 1989 effectively does away with the local authority's right to take wardship proceedings for the purpose of taking care and control, except with leave of the court under Section 100 (4), where exceptional circumstances have to be satisfied.

Alternatives to care or supervision (Schedule 2, Part 1, para. 5)

The local authority has power to assist 'another person' to obtain alternative accommodation where it appears that the child is likely to suffer ill-treatment at the hands of that person if she continues living on the premises. This may include financial help.

Representation of the child (Part IV, Section 41)

The court is empowered to appoint a guardian *ad litem* to safeguard the interests of the child, or to appoint a solicitor to represent her if it seems to be in the child's best interests to do so.

Rules regarding evidence given by children (Part XII, 96 and 97)

Even if it is thought that the child does not understand the meaning of an oath, her evidence can still be heard if the court is satisfied that the child understands her duty to speak the truth (Section 96 (3)).

The Lord Chancellor may make provision for the admissibility of evidence which would otherwise be inadmissible under the rule of law regarding hearsay. This provision appears to open the door to the possibility of video-recorded interviews with the child being acceptable in evidence, although this may still not be the case in criminal proceedings.

The court may also choose to hear cases regarding children in private session and to impose reporting restrictions.

Civil proceedings

There are several courses of action open to the abused child under civil procedures, either instead of or as well as any criminal action taken by the Crown Prosecution Service.

The law of torts

The child may sue the abuser under the law of torts, obtaining redress by way of damages. This law includes the offences of 'trespass to the person', 'false imprisonment', and 'intentional mental distress' – some or all of which may be particularly relevant in the case of child sexual abuse.

Clearly it is of no value to bring this kind of action if the abuser has no assets.

The advantages of this kind of action include the fact that the standard of proof is probably less rigorous, in that a decision in civil actions is reached on 'a balance of probabilities' rather than 'beyond reasonable doubt', which is the standard required in criminal proceedings.

The rules regarding admissible evidence from children are also probably less strict in civil actions. Although independent corroboration of the child's statements is still important, it is possible for a civil case to succeed without it.

The first step is to consult a solicitor who will advise whether the action is likely to succeed, although the decision as to whether to proceed must always be the child's own.

If there has already been a successful criminal prosecution, the chances of success are extremely high.

A guardian *ad litem* should be appointed for the child. This can be a family member, friend, or counsellor.

Legal aid should then be applied for. Since children under 16 are no longer means tested on their parents' income, this is likely to be granted.

It is preferable to institute the action as soon as possible after the event, but it will not be excluded on grounds of time if it is brought before the child is 21. There is no lower age limit for such an action, but it may be invalidated if the child is too young to understand her duty to speak the truth.

Medical and psychiatric reports will be helpful in proving not only liability, but also the extent of physical and emotional harm to the child. This in turn will determine the amount of damages awarded. The award may take into account the possible loss of future earnings (perhaps as a result of academic failure) and the cost of continuing therapy.

Injunctions

The child may apply for an injunction to restrain the abuser from 'assaulting, molesting, or harming' the applicant. This is useful where it is important to ensure that the abuser, not the child, leaves the family home.

A guardian *ad litem* should be appointed, and a legal aid application made. Legal aid for this kind of action can be obtained quickly, and the injunction can often be granted within two days.

Evidence can be given by affidavit, and the child is not required to give evidence in court.

If the abuser flouts the injunction, he is guilty of contempt, and may go to prison.

Delay between the event and the action may prejudice the application.

It is also possible for a parent and child to apply jointly for an injunction against an abuser, although where the abuser is the other parent, this presupposes a breakdown of the marital relationship. It may be useful where the mother fears reprisals from a violent partner.

The Criminal Injuries Compensation Board

This is composed of a committee of eminent lawyers, and is empowered to award compensation to the victim of any crime.

The board must be satisfied as to the proof of the crime, and the proof of the damage suffered as a result.

It is obliged to make an award equivalent to that which might be made by a civil court, although if the child is not represented by a lawyer, the amount may in practice be lower.

There is an 18-month time limit from the offence to the claim.

This provision is helpful if the abuser has no funds, or in providing the balance of payment if the total amount of civil damages cannot be met by the abuser.

Criminal prosecution of the offender

The perpetrator may be charged with a variety of offences under the Offence Against the Persons Act 1861 or the Sexual Offences Act 1956.

Charges will not usually be made if the child is unwilling to give evidence, or unless there is some independent corroboration of the child's statement. However, in rare cases, the Crown Prosecution Service can insist on the child giving evidence if it is thought that it is in the public interest for a prosecution to take place.

The police may decide to consult the Crown Prosecution Service as to whether a case has a reasonable chance of success. While awaiting a decision, the suspected offender may be released on police bail without being charged. Alternatively, he may be charged and brought in front of the magistrates, who will decide if bail is appropriate, and, if so, the amount required, until a trial date is set.

Indictable offences, or those which would normally entail a sentence of five years or more on the first conviction, will generally be tried before a jury in the Crown Court. However, even in the case of summary offences, normally heard in the Magistrates Court, the defendant may elect for a jury trial in the Crown Court.

Video-taped evidence from the child can be admitted in the Crown Court, but this is entirely at the discretion of the judge. Even if it is agreed, the defence has a right to cross-examine the child. Again, at the judge's discretion, this can be done by a video link if it is thought to be too distressing for the child to give evidence in open court. However, not all Crown Courts have facilities for this procedure — only 14 Crown Courts in the UK are suitably equipped at the present time.

Sentencing usually entails a prison term, and few facilities are available for treatment while the offender is detained. The Portman Clinic in London and the Gracewell Clinic in Birmingham offer treatment to offenders not in custody. It is to be hoped that better provisions can be made in the future.

Resources

Books for children

Alice doesn't Babysit Any More. Kevin McGovern, Mulbacker, 1985.

Back in the First Person. Kathy Page, Virago Press, 1986.
   Suitable for teens upwards.

Come and Tell me. Helen Hollick. Dinosaur Publications, 1986.
   Suitable for ages 3–6. Warning of approaches by strangers.

Don't Tell Your Mother. Tom Hart. Quartet Books, 1981.
   Suitable for teens upwards.

I Can't Talk About It. Doris Sandford, Multnomah, 1986.

I'm Glad I Told Mum! Jenny Hessell & Mandy Nelson, Beaver Books, 1988.

It's OK to Say No: Parent/Child Manual for the Protection of Children. Robin Lennet & Bob Crane. Thorsons, 1986.
   Ages 4–7.

Look Back, Stride Forward. Miriam Saphira. Papers, 1989.

Mousie. Khadj Rouf. Children's Society, 1989.
   Suitable for very young children.

My Feelings. Marcia K. Morgan, Equal Just. Con., 1984.

No is Not Enough. Caren Adams, Jennifer Fay, & Jan Loreen Martin. Collins, 1989.
   Suitable for teenagers.

No More Secrets for Me. O. Wachter. Little, Brown & Co., 1984.
   Suitable for ages 4–8.

Porky. Deborah Moggach. Penguin Books, 1984.
   Teenage or adult.

Push Me, Pull Me. Sandra Chick. Women's Press 'Livewire', 1987.
   Suitable for teenagers.

Rabbit's Golden Rule Book. Pam Adams. Child's Play, 1988.
Suitable for very young children.

Safe, Strong and Streetwise. Helen Benedict. Hodder & Stoughton, 1988.
Suitable for teenagers.

Secrets, (White Families). Khadj Rouf. Children's Soc., 1989.

Secrets. (Black Families). Khadj Rouf. Children's Soc., 1989.

Take Care! Preventing Child Sexual Abuse. Clodagh Corcoran. Poolbeg Press, 1987.

Tom Doesn't Visit Us Any More. Mary Leah Otto. Women's Press of Canada, 1988.

Too Close Encounters and What to Do About Them. Rosemary Stones. Piccadilly Press, 1987.
Suitable for teenagers.

We Can Say No! David Pithers & Sarah Green. Hutchinson, 1986.
Suitable for ages 3–6.

Willow Street Kids. Michele Elliott. Andre Deutsch, 1986 & Pan Books, 1987.
Suitable for ages 7–11. Based on true stories.

Books for Adults

The ABC of Child Abuse Work. Jean Moore. Gower Publ. Co., 1985.

Adults Molested as Children: A Survivors' Manual for Women & Men. E. Bear & P. Dimrock. First Society Press, 1988.

Ask Any Woman: London Enquiry into Rape and Sexual Assault. Ruth E. Hall. Falling Wall Press, 1985.

The Battle and the Backlash. David Hechler. Lexington Books, 1989.
An examination of policies relating to child abuse in the USA.

The Best-Kept Secret: Sexual Abuse of Children. F. Rush. Prentice Hall, 1980.

Betrayal of Innocence: Incest and its Devastation. S. Forward & C. Buck. Penguin, 1981.

Beyond Sexual Abuse. D. Jehu, M. Gazan, & C. Klassen. Wiley, 1989.

By Silence Betrayed: The Sexual Abuse of Children in America. John Crewdson. Harper & Row, 1988.
A journalistic account of recent developments in the USA.

Child Abuse: The Developing Child. Ruth S. Kempe & C. Henry Kempe. Open Books, Fontana, 1979.

Children and the Law: Young People and Their Rights. Maggie Rae. Longman, 1986.

Children, Parents and the Law. E. Rudinger. Consumers' Association, 1985 (currently out of print).

Child Sexual Abuse. R. J. Parter. The Ciba Foundation, Tavistock Publications, 1984.

Child Sexual Abuse: New Theory. David Finkelhor. Free Press, 1984.

Child Sexual Abuse. Danya Glaser & Stephen Frosh. Macmillan Educ. Books, 1988.

Child Sexual Abuse: Listening, Hearing and Validating the Experiences of Children. Harry Blagg (ed.). (NSPCC) Longman, 1989.

Child Sexual Abuse: A Hope for Healing. M. Hancock & K. B. Mains. Highland Books, 1987.

Child Sexual Abuse within the Family. Ruth Porter (ed.). Tavistock, 1984.

The Color Purple. A. Walker. Pocket Books, 1982.

The Common Secret: Sexual Abuse of Children and Adolescents. R. S. Kempe & C. H. Kempe. Freeman Press. 1984.

Conspiracy of Silence. Sandra Butler. Volcano Press, 1986.

The Courage to Heal. Ellen Bass & Laura Davis. Harper & Row, 1988.
   For adult survivors.

Cry Hard and Swim. Jacqueline Spring. Virago Banks, 1987.

Daddy's Girl. C. V. Allen. Berkeley Books, 1980.

Diagnosis of Child Sexual Abuse: Guidance for Doctors. DHSS. HMSO Publ., 1988.

Don't! A Woman's Word. Elly Danica. Women's Press, 1989.

Don't Tell Your Mother. Tom Hart. Quartet Books, 1981.
   Suitable for teenage to adult.

Early Prediction and Prevention of Child Abuse. K. Browne, C. Davies & P. Stratton (eds). John Wiley & Sons Ltd, 1988.

Father–Daughter Incest. Judith Herman. Harvard University Press, 1981.

Father–Daughter Rape. Elizabeth Ward. Women's Press, 1984.

Father's Days: A True Story of Incest. K. Brady. Dell Books, 1979.

Focus on Child Abuse: Medical, Legal and Social Work Perspectives. Allan Levy (ed.). Hawksmere, 1989.

For Your Child's Sake: Understanding Sexual Abuse. Miriam Saphira. Heinemann Reed, 1990.

For Your Own Good: The Roots of Violence in Child Rearing. Alice Miller. Virago Press, 1987.

Fostering the Battered and Abused Child. Emily Jean McFadden. Institute for the Study of Children and Families, Eastern Michigan University, 1982.

Handbook of Clinical Intervention in Child Abuse. Suzanne M. Sgroi. Lexington Books, 1982.

Home Is Where the Hurt Is: Guidance for all Victims of Sexual Abuse in the Home and for Those who Support Them. Janine Turner. Thornsons, 1989.

If I Should Die Before I Wake. Michele Morris. Black Swan, 1984.

I Know Why the Caged Bird Sings. Maya Angelou. Virago Press, 1984.

Incest and Sexuality: A Guide to Understanding and Healing. Wendy Maltz & Beverley Holman. Lexington Books, 1987. For teenage & adult survivors including information for partners.

Incest: Fact and Myth (2nd edn). Sarah Nelson. Stramullion Press, 1987.

I Never Told Anyone. Ellen Bass & Louise Thornton. Harper & Row, 1983.

In Our Experience. S. Krzowski & P. Land (eds). Women's Press, 1988.

In Our Own Hands: A Woman's Book of Self-Help Therapy. S. Ernst & L. Goodison. Women's Press, 1981.

Inside Scars: Incest Recovery as Told by a Survivor and Her Therapist. S. L. Sisk & C. F. Hoffman. Pandora Press. 1987.

Integrated Treatment of Child Sexual Abuse. Henry Giaretto. Science & Behaviour Books Inc., 1982.

Interviewing the Sexually Abused Child. David Jones & Mary McQuiston. Gaskell, 1988.

Keeping Safe: A Practical Guide to Talking with Children. Michelle Elliott. New English Library, 1988. A common sense guide for parents.

The Lasting Effect of Child Sexual Abuse. Gail Wyatt & Gloria Powell (eds). Sage Publications, 1988.

Michelle Remembers. Michelle Smith & Lawrence Pazder. Sphere Paperbacks, 1982. A personal account of a survivor of ritual abuse.

The Mothers' Book: How to Survive the Incest of Your Child. Carolyn M. Byerly. Kendall Hunt, 1985.

My Father's House: Memoir of Incest and Healing. Sylvia Fraser. Virago, 1989.

No Longer a Victim. C.-A. Matthews. Acorn Press, 1986.

No More Secrets: Protecting Your Child from Sexual Assault. Caren Adams & Jennifer Fay. Impact Publishers, 1983.

Nursery Crimes: Sexual Abuse in Day Care. David Finkelhor, *et al*. Sage Publications, 1989.

Outgrowing the Pain. Iliana Gil. Launch Press, 1983.
  For adult survivors.

Reclaiming Our Lives. Carol Poston & Karen Lison. Little, Brown & Co., 1989.
  For adult survivors.

The Report of the Inquiry into Child Abuse in Cleveland 1987. HMSO, 1988.

The Safe Child Book. Sherryll Kerns Kraiser. Futura Publications, 1986.

Secret Survivors. E. Sue Blume. John Wiley & Sons Ltd; 1990.

The Secret Trauma: Incest in the Lives of Girls and Women. Diana Russell (ed.). Basic Books, 1986.

Sexual Abuse of Young Children. Kee MacFarlane & Jill Waterman. Cassell, 1988.

Sexual Exploitation. Diana Russell. Sage Publications, 1984.

Sexually Abused Children and Their Families. P. B. Mrazek & C. H. Kempe (eds). Pergamon Press, 1981.

Sexually Victimized Children. David Finkelhor. Free Press, 1979.

Sexual Victimization. D. J. West. Gower Press, 1985.

The Silent Children. Linda Tschirart Sandford. McGraw Hill, 1982.

A Source Book on Child Sexual Abuse. David Finkelhor. Sage Publications, 1986.

Step by Step: Sixteen Steps towads Legally Sound Sexual Abuse Investigations. Jan Hindman. Alexandria Assoc., 1987.

The Story of Ruth. Morton Schatzman. Penguin, 1982.

Suffer the Child. Judith Spencer. Pocket Books, 1989.
  Deals with ritual abuse.

Surviving Child Sexual Abuse. Liz Hall & Siobhan Lloyd. Falmer Press, 1989.

That Looks Like a Nice House. C. E. Wynne. Launch Press, 1987.

This is about Incest. Margaret Randall. Firebrand Books, 1987.

Thou Shalt Not Be Aware: Society's Betrayal of the Child. A. Miller. Pluto, 1984.

Treating Child Sex Offenders and Victims: A Practical Guide. Anna C. Salter. Sage Publications, 1989.

Treating Sexually Abused Children and Their Families. Beverley James & Maria Nasjleti. Consulting Psychologist Press, 1983.

Treatment of Adult Survivors of Child Abuse. E. Gil. Launch Press, 1988.

Unofficial Secrets: Child Abuse — The Cleveland Case. Beatrix Campbell. Virago, 1988.

Voices in the Night. Toni McNaron & Yarrow Morgan (eds). Cleis Press 1984.

Woman's Experience of Sex. Sheila Kitzinger. Pelican, 1985.

Working Together. DHSS. HMSO, 1988.
   A guide for inter-agency co-operation in the protection of children from abuse.

Working with Sexually Abused Boys. J. Christopherson, Helen Armstrong, & Anne Hollows (eds). National Children's Bureau, 1989.

Leaflets

Being a Proper Stranger
   National Children's Home
   85c Highbury Park, London N5 1UD
   Free

Guide for Families with Children in Care: 101 Questions and Answers
   Parents Against Injustice
   2 Plegdon Green, Henham, Bishops Stortford, Herts.
   Send £1.50 & large SAE with 59p postage

How to Help Them Stay Safe
   Kidscape
   82 Brook St, London W1Y 1YG
   Free with large SAE

If in Doubt, Shout
   Childwatch
   60 Beck Road, Everthrope, Brough, Humberside
   Price 50p

Keeping Your Children Out of Danger
   National Children's Home
   85c Highbury Park, London N5 1UD
   Free

Protect Your Child
NSPCC
67 Saffon Hill, London EC1N 8RS
Free

Videos for children

Better Safe than Sorry, 1,2, & 3 (14 minutes)
Educational Media International, 25 Boileau Road, London W5 3AL
Feeling Yes, Feeling No (35 minutes)
Educational Media International, 25 Boileau Road, London W5 3AL
Have Fun – Take Care (20 minutes)
Community Involvement Team. Tooting Police Station, Mitcham Rd, London SW17 9QJ (tel. 081–672–9922)
Kids Can Say No (20 minutes)
Skippon Video Associates Ltd, 43 Drury Lane, London WC2
No More Secrets (13 minutes)
Educational Media International, 25 Boileau Road, London W5 3AL
Now I Can Tell You My Secret (15 minutes)
Walt Disney Educational Services, 31–2 Soho Square, London W1V 6AP
Say No to Strangers (18 minutes)
Home Office Film
Shown by local police on request by schools.
Stranger Danger (12 minutes)
Thames Valley Police, Police Headquarters, Kidlington, Oxford OX5 2NX, (tel. 0865–846000)
Shown in schools on request
Strong Kids, Safe Kids (38 minutes)
CIC Video, UIP House, 45 Beadon Road, London W6
Time to Talk (20 minutes)
Samaritans, 17 Uxbridge Rd, Slough SL1 1SN (tel. 0753–32713)

Videos for adults

Adam (92 minutes)
Michael Tuchner. Odyssey, CBS Fox Video Ltd, Unit 1,

Perivale Industrial Park, Greenford, Middlesex UB6 7RU
(tel. 081–997–2552)

Breaking Silence (58 minutes)
Theresa Tollini/Future Education Flms, Albany Videos, The
Albany, Douglas Way, London SE8 4AG

Child Molestation: Breaking the Silence (20 minutes)
Walt Disney Educational Services, 31–2 Soho Square, London
W1V 6AP

Secret Sounds Screaming: The Sexual Abuse of Children
(25 minutes)
Ayoka Chenzira, Albany Videos, The Albany, Douglas Way,
London SE8 4AG

Self-Esteem and Personal Safety
Eileen Vizard, Tavistock Film Unit, Tavistock Institute of Human
Relations, Belsize Park Road, London NW3

Sexual Abuse of Children (90 minutes)
Audio Visual Service, University of Leeds, Leeds LS2 9JT
(tel. 0532–431751)

*Sexually Abused Children: The Sensitive Medical Examination and
Management*
RSM Services Ltd, Film & Television Unit, 1 Wimple St, London
W1M 8AE

Talking with Sexually Abused Children (3 videos – 90 minutes)
Audio Visual Service, University of Leeds, Leeds LS2 9JT
(tel. 0532–431751)

Through the Eyes of a Child (30 minutes)
Florence Hallum Prevention of Child Abuse Fund (UK), 36–8
Peckham Road, London SE5 8QR

Helping agencies

Childline
50 Studd Street, London N1 0QJ. 071–239–1000 Also
Freephone 0800–111 and Freepost 1111, London EC4 4BB
Confidential 24-hour telephone counselling service for children

Child Helpline
0742–886886
Telephone advice and support for victims of abuse in the
Sheffield area

The Children's Legal Centre
20 Compton Terrace, London N1 2UN 081–359–6251
Advice about law and policy affecting children

Family Contact Line
061–941–4066 10 a.m. to 10 p.m.
Telephone listening service for families; also provides nursery facilities

Gracewell Clinic. Director: Ray Wyre
81 Walker's Heath Road, King's Norton, Birmingham B38 0AN.
021–433–3888
Family counselling and therapy for offenders

Incest Crisis Line
32 Newbury Close, Northolt, Middlesex UB5 4JF. 081–422–5100
Voluntary counselling service to victims and professionals offered by survivors: 24-hour telephone service and local contacts when available.

In Support of Sexually Abused Children
Angela Rivera, PO Box 526, London NW6 1SU. 081–202–3024
Support for sexually abused children and their parents

International Conferences on Incest and Related Problems
ICIRP Conference Office, 101 Harley St, London W1N 1DF.
071–935–1811
Yearly conferences held in London; also counselling courses in London and Switzerland

International Network Against Incest and Child Sexual Abuse
c/o Virginia Klein, PhD. 18 South Cadillac Drive, Somerville, New Jersey 08876, USA
To facilitate international exchange of information and creation of helping agencies

International Society for Prevention of Child Abuse and Neglect
c/o Pergamon Journals Ltd (att. B.J. Smith), Headington Hill Hall, Oxford OX3 0BW. 0865–64881

Kidscape
82 Brook St, London W1Y 1YG. 071–493–9845
Free 16-page guide for parents: advice on developing children's defence strategies

Lifeline – Family help for abuse within the home
   PO Box 251, Marlborough, Wiltshire SN8 1EA. 0793–731286
   Also 091–413–9566 and 0283–226060
   24-hour service for abused and abusers: individual, telephone or
   family counselling, also self-help groups

London Rape Crisis Centre
   PO Box 69, London WC1X 9NJ. 071–837–1600 (24 hours)
   071–278–3956 (office hours)
   24-hour telephone advice for women and girls who have been
   raped

London Youth Advisory Centre
   26 Prince of Wales Rd, Kentish Town, London NW5 3LG.
   071–267–4792
   Counselling for young people aged 12–25 on a variety of
   problems; self-referral welcome

Mothers of Abused Children
   Chris Strickland, 0965–31432 (Cumbria)
   Telephone support line for mothers

National Children's Bureau
   8 Wakeley St, London EC1V 7QE. 071–278–9441
   Liaison between statutory and voluntary bodies concerned with
   child care: information service for professional workers

National Children's Home
   85 Highbury Park, London N5 1UD. 071–226–2033
   Individual counselling service, and information for parents and
   professionals. Regional 'Careline' phone-in services – see local
   directory for numbers

National Society for the Prevention of Cruelty to Children
   67 Saffron Hill, London EC1N 8RS. 071–242–1626
   Local Child Protection Teams offering 24-hour advice and
   intervention; training programmes and information for professionals

Organization for Parents Under Stress (OPUS)
   106 Godstone Rd, Whyteleafe, Surrey CR3 0EB. 081–645–0469
   Network of self-help groups for parents: operates a 24-hour
   answerphone for distress calls

Parents Against Injustice (PAIN)
   Conifers, 2 Plegdon Green, Henham, Bishops Stortford,
   Hertfordshire CM22 6BN. 0279–850545

Offers advice and support to parents and carers mistakenly suspected of child abuse: 24-hour counselling service; literature resource centre

Parents Anonymous
6 Manor Gardens, London N7 6LA. 071–263–8918 6 p.m. to 6 a.m.
Offers help to parents who fear they may abuse their children

The Portman Clinic
8 Fitzjohns Avenue, London NW3 5NA. 071–794–8262/5
National Health Service facility offering out-patient treatment for sexual offenders

SAFE
Sue Hutchinson, 0980–623137
Telephone support line for survivors of ritual and cult abuse

St Christopher's Fellowship
53 Warwick Rd. London SW5 1AD. 071–370–2522
Residential therapeutic centre for severely abused children aged 5–10; care projects for older and homeless children

Samaritans
17 Uxbridge Road, Slough SL1 1SN. 0753–32713
24-hour listening service (*see* local telephone book for numbers)

Sexual Abuse Child Consultancy Service (SACCS)
40 Meole Crescent, Meole Brace, Shrewsbury SY3 9ET. 0743–236433
Skills training and consultancy to professionals: individual therapeutic help for abused children; catalogue of books and toys available by mail order

Spectrum Incest Intervention Project
7 Endymion Road, London N4 1EE. 071–348–0196
Works with victims, survivors, and perpetrators: educational and training workshops

Standing Committee on Sexually Abused Children (SCOSAC)
73 St Charles Square, London W10 6EJ. 081–960–6376
London network providing training and resource centre for professionals and voluntary workers; no counselling or advice to the general public

Touchline
    0532–45777 9.30 a.m. to 9.30 p.m. weekdays
    Telephone listening service for anyone who has been abused

Victims' Help Line
    St Leonards, Nuttall St. London N1 5LZ. Office: 071–729–1226;
    Helpline: 071–729–1252
    24-hour confidential counselling for victims of any crime; no formal
    links with the police

Victim Suport Scheme
    17a Electric Lane, London SW9 8LA. 071–326–1084
    A nationwide network of support groups offering help to victims of
    violence and crime

Index